Legs Spread
Heart Open

- ♀ -

A Gush of Poems

Email: bylottiewoodward@gmail.com
Youtube: By Lottie Woodward
Facebook: By Lottie Woodward
Website: www.bylottiewoodward.co.uk

ISBN: 9781729136058

Dedicated to my friends
at Katie Fitzgerald's, who
encourage me write and read aloud,
and stay up late and drink too much.

And to Elliott,
whose passing brought us together.

Introduction

- ♀ -

This collection gushed out of me during a challenging period of my life. The beauty of pain, however, is that it drives me to my laptop to make sense of it through poetry. And there is an additional bonus. Now I am a *woman of a certain age*, so I no longer give a shit. I write what I like.

I don't care if the neighbours find things out about me. I'm not bothered about embarrassing my children. It's payback for the tantrums they had at the checkout.

What gushed out was not so much an angry rant from a menopausal woman (although there is some of that), but a brutally honest look at the world through the eyes of someone who appreciates that pain is growth. However difficult it feels to get out of bed in the morning, this world is a beautifully unpredictable, stunning, maddening and magical place.

I hate missing out, so however challenging, I'm grateful to be on the crazy rollercoaster of Life. After all, at some time during the 1960s, there was a one in three *billion* chance my parents, from different continents, met when they did. Out of 100,000 *billion* sperm, *one* fought its way to the egg, released from a store of literally hundreds of thousands as my mother sang along to Elvis. The odds of me being here are infinitesimally small, of being a poet, smaller still. I have nearly 200,000 English words to pick in almost limitless combinations.

I picked these. I hope you enjoy them.

Part One

- ♀ -

Painful Days

To Chloe, because you understand

Chloe

A living Russian doll.
The outside is fragile
But inside fragility, there is strength;
Inside strength, there is beauty;
Inside beauty, there is wisdom
And inside wisdom, there is humour.
Layer upon layer; style upon style,
A multi-faceted, hugely talented,
Bowie-loving, edge cutting
Russian doll.
Loving, loyal, exquisitely protective,
Does not suffer fools; fiercely selective.
So many dolls with which to contend
But each one inside, I call friend.

ZELDA

I want to tell you about Zelda

She was married to the writer, F Scott Fitzgerald

The original flapper

Man trapper

Gossip and scandal a-plenty

Party girl of the roaring 20s

Wild, free-spirited, sensual, unfiltered

She swam naked, walked barefoot and cut off her hair

She could drink men under the table anywhere

But back then, women were meant to be docile, Southern Belles

Some even thought she was a witch from hell

So they shut her away in an asylum

Put her in straight jackets and locked her in cells

Her journals tell of the screams and the smells

And they gave her shock therapy

Repeatedly, repeatedly

She died in a fire, locked in a cell

Unable to escape

Her life fascinates me

And perhaps this is why

Women in asylums were

Beaten, raped, starved and abused

They underwent years of shock therapy

And had their clitorises removed

Many were not ill, but had issues

Like postnatal depression, or were sexually promiscuous,

or had powerful husbands who wanted them out of the way

Old women, young women, some only teenage

Only when their stories went public

Did the system change

At 17, I was the party girl of the punk era

Wild, free-spirited, sensual, unfiltered

I swam naked, walked barefoot and cut off my hair

I could drink every man in this room under the table

But then lampposts began talking to me

Giving me messages from Mars

It was so real, that if I think about it too long, even now

Part of me thinks it was true

I didn't know what to do

My brain is broken, I told the doctor

He said, no. You have bipolar disorder

And you're going to be fine

You will learn to manage it

There are drugs to help

You can work, have children, live a life

It will be alright

And...with work, it is

But when things get bleak

When I fall through the gaps in the pavement

Or destroy my life because... it might be fun

I think about Zelda Fitzgerald

Just 20 years before I was born

She burnt like a witch

In a cell

I wouldn't have stood a chance
I know there are others who share the same
I can't stop your pain or remove the shame
Or change the state you are in
On days you want to peel off your skin
But I think of Zelda
Beautiful, beautiful Zelda
I'm so sorry no one came
Women like her took the pain
So women like me can be free
Do you see
What an amazing thing to do
For that, Zelda, I thank you

Apron Strings♥♥

While I wasn't looking, my children grew up
and now they've flown the nest,
even my baby talks of leaving home and university
and part of me, part of me, feels excited
that when I walk through that door
the house will look exactly as I left it.

Part of me...

But the heart of me, oh, that's beating,
because I'm a mum, that's who I am,
and a single mum at that.
It's always been us against the world
and no, I couldn't provide the big house
and no, I didn't buy them smart cars,
so what can I give as a parting gift
as they head off into life?

Well, I could finally...

tell them who their father is.
I don't mean the guy with the...
They know who that is,
and I don't mean God the father
because each to their own,
as a family, we cope alone.

But before they walk away
and tear off those apron strings,
I'll tell them; your father is the sun
and your mother is the moon
and this crazy world in the middle, it's yours,
all yours,

all you need to do is reach out your hand and take it.

And it's a good world, a great world -
most of the time.
But sometimes, sometimes, it will treat you bad.
It has a way of knocking you down
and standing you up and dusting you off
just to knock you down again,
and sometimes life is hard and love is hard
and no, there won't be money to go party, be arty,
play music, go travelling or even pay the gas bill

and I don't have any spare, so you're on your own.

But when life has bowled you down and stood you up
and bowled you down again, this world is still yours.
And not all days will be like that;
Not all days are black.
There'll be days with the sun on your back;
days when you look at the lines on the palms of your hand
and join the dots to freedom;

days when insects hover the meadows
like small galaxies;
when the beauty of a frosted web will move you to tears.
There'll be sledging days and weddings days
And lazy days; new baby days,
new homes, new jobs, new loves...

New loves...*I* was their first love.

Days when you look in the mirror at your own eyes
and say, 'Yes! I know who I am and I know where I live.
I live on this crazy world and it's mine,
all mine.'
So you just remember, when life knocks you down,
On days when the cuckoos come circling
and you cannot protect the precious eggs you made,

that Mum is waiting, behind that door,
in a house that is oh, so tidy,
and I will stitch those apron strings together

and throw them out and pull you in,
with a full kettle and a bottle of Jack Daniels,
because Jack solves everything, right?

Okay, I know Jack can't solve everything

but when the coffee has failed and the Jack has failed,
I have two things left, I have my arms,
and it doesn't matter where you are, because a mama's arms
are strong enough and long enough to reach around the planet.
So, you just remember, when life treats you bad,
that your father is the sun and your mother is the moon
and you, you are a child of a star, that's who you are,
and wherever I am, in this world or the next,
there'll always be a bottle of Jack
and there'll always be two arms,

because I'm your mum.

Beauty & the Beast

If you view it in a different way,
close one eye, catch it
through the tears in your lashes –
The Beast is a beauteous thing,
the fragile wing
of a butterfly crushed underfoot,
muddied, dead, but never less than it was.
Yesterday, it flicked the lavender
and licked the buddleia, reflecting spring.
Let its echo sing from the pavement
where its flight of fancy ends.
If you can try, try to see it in a different way,
the Beauty, hope and expectation,
the ordinary, you thought would
stay ordinary, does not die
but hovers in the hedgerow
where it always exists,
to climb out of its chrysalis
and in its curt encounter
make our lives worthwhile.
We cannot see the Beauty
if we do not know The Beast.

Empty

I cannot **write** today,
For poetry does not lurk
In empty lines of silence.
Nothing is observed where nothing exists,
There are no verses in the void.

I cannot *feel* today,
For poetry needs voices
In lengthy vines of perchance.
Nothing consists where silence persists,
There is no meaning here employed.

I will write tomorrow.
For poetry's a cycle
Of plenty days and empty days.
Nothing last forever, silence, never,

My pen **SHOUTS** once silence is destroyed.

Fly and Fall

Call me Bipolar
Watch me make, create
Soar the distant lie
Of a rainbow sky
Guide you to your core
So the greenish sly
Of a flower's eye
Stakes you to the floor
And slaughters you with beauty

My name is Bipolar
Watch me hate, dictate
Hear me roar
To the hungry cry
As the carrion high
Circle your internal war
See me horrify
And amplify
And break against the door
Of sanity and reason

My name is Bipolar
A world of extremes
Washed out grey shadows
To kaleidoscope dreams
What does it mean?
To one day walk with angels
In the prism of a raindrop's sigh
The next day fall to death
To my hideous lullaby

Holes

I walk the wall of the ancient bridge,
Bare toes grip the red, wet brick.
Beneath me, the river is dark and cold,

Deep • holes • in • the • bed, deep holes •

I imagine the water choking my throat
As I gulp the juice of the Severn.
I watch the water run under the bridge,
So much water under the bridge,
A lifetime of water runs under the bridge,

Over • the • holes, deep • holes •

There on the bank, a girl waves her hand,
Bare feet on the wet, grounded grass.
Her face is as white as river foam
As she beckons me home, beckons me home.

I know that pale face, it's familiar to me,
I saw it today in the mirror.
I watch the water dry under the bridge,
No more water under the bridge.

She holds out her hand and the river's flow...
Stops dead.

Mirror Pieces

Who is this woman with the sad, sad eyes,
stained by time that pools beneath the lids?
The furrowed lines of painful days
plough her brow and pucker at her lips
in half circles like the dark side of moons
that lovers have neglected,
beetle legs swarm in the crease of her eyes
in the space where stale tears have collected.

What will I see if I raise, raise my fist
and smash the mirror to shards?
What will I find if I sink to the floor
to remake the picture, part by part?
Will the girl with the smile, the hopes
and the dreams, in the splinters be reflected?
In a different order, will I see
the life I *could* have selected?

The Secret

It's a secret
No one talks about
Blades on skin
Crimson blood
Drips like rain
Drips, drips like rain
Let's us know we're still alive
That we still feel pain

They call us freaks
Attention seekers
Drama queens
We hide our scars in shame
Roll about on silent screams
And our blood drips
Drip, drip, blood drips

We are not cutters
Or slicers
Or self harmers
We are *people*
Who found a way
To ease the pain
To keep our souls alive
Manage our feelings
Until we find a better way

We hurt no one
We internalise the pain
And turn it only on ourselves
But there is another way
We do not have to be a whisper

We can speak OUT

LIFT our heads
ASK for help
DEMAND understanding
Support one another
Take away the stigma
Take away the shame
Educate the public
Who could
If they would
Support us with our pain

Part Two

- ♀ -

Positive Days

To Trina, for warm
welcomes and jaw-dropping stories

Happy Birthday Trina

There's a **<u>woman</u>** here tonight, called Trina
Wow, have you seen her? Let's just take stock of the posh frock
Sixty today, but no has-been
Oh no, she's a mean, lean, vodka machine that runs on nicotine; a queen
This pub is her palace, the bar her limousine
Never forgotten once seen, that's Trine

There's a **<u>warrior</u>** here tonight, called Trina
And 'though some might say she's a dreamer
With banners unfurled, she fights for a better world
The animals, the underdog and the broken, and, yes some say she's outspoken
But she's just very open, it's not just a token
She really has awoken to what goes on in our world

There's a **<u>minx</u>** here tonight, called Trina
A punky little screamer, goes like a paddle steamer
With make-up on and pouted lips, the music's on, she shakes those hips
Let's be clear, we don't know how she made it here!
She sailed through the 27 club, was dirty at thirty
Naughty at forty, nifty at fifty and so sexy and sixty

And the years pass, still there with her vodka glass
Smoking like a chimney, wearing something flimsy
Swearing like a trooper and looking like a cougar

There's a **friend** here tonight, called Trina
And I couldn't be keener to wish her lots of love
And blessings from above.
A woman, a hostess, a wife with the mostess
Words of wisdom and serenity wrapped in obscenity
A kind word and a listening ear for all who venture
here
So, Trina Keane, kissing machine
Happy birthday my old chum, and many, many more
to come

EGGS FOR SALE

I stopped for eggs today
On the A450
In a crocodile of cars
Impatient to be home...
Hot
Reflecting on the day
Concerned about tomorrow
Light on the dashboard winking
Stop blinking!
Flirting with my worry
(it's a bad month for money)
What should I cook?
How do I look?
And why does my left shoe hurt?

I saw the sign for

EGGS

Turned on a whim
Up a twisting, gravelled drive
A handmade sign bid me...

WELCOME

Pots spaced the edge
Grass, fresh cut, lush,
Bee hives by the hedge
Wind chimes tinkling
Glass panes twinkling
In a whitewashed dwelling
Where the eggs were selling
An old collie smiled
Where the logs were piled
And an old man stood in his wellies

He called me, *my lover*
And named the hens
Who laid for me
Offered me tea...

Peace.

I took the milky drink
And poked around his garden
He knew every plant
Every shrub and tree
Shown to me
And petty worries ebbed away
It really was a lovely day
I shouldn't worry
About work and money
And strangely, my left shoe no longer hurt.

Heaven

Heaven

I find myself in a strange town,
driving a car I do not own,
no memory of how I got here,
so I pull into a car park to find someone,
anyone, to explain. ♪♫

The sun is sinking into sunset glory
as sweet beats pulse from a club.
Red, orange, purple lights
flashing at the windows,
entice me to a party. ♪♫

I'm surprised to find Lemmy on the door.
"Sold out," he says, as I approach.
"You need a pass, baby girl."
"This one?" I pull out a
golden ticket I didn't know was there.
"Hey, you're guest of honour." He waves me past.
"And drinks are on the house." ♪♫

Inside, it is dangerously dark and sleazy.
The crowd cheer the band, who play
their souls out on stage.
The barman is velvet black
with dreads down to the floor.
"Whisky on the rocks?" He smiles
in a *see you later* kind of way. ♪♫

I notice Bowie chatting to Bob Marley,
who winks and hands me the never ending spliff.
In a corner, Hendrix talks politics to Janis Joplin
and Elvis moves his pelvis to the beat.
I join the crowd, infected by their mood
as they cheer and clap and wave. ♪♫

The crowd are people that I know -
old school friends who have passed,
an English teacher who turned *me* into a wordsmith
and Gran, dancing in her apron and her slippers;
good men I walked away from
and better ones, who walked away from me.
All my nearest and my dearest,
loving the music,
loving the band. ♪♫

Jesus Christ is on guitar, laying down a dirty riff,
Allah sings the blues
and Shiva destroys us with his sax solo
and at the back, a big fat Buddha
drums funky fills in time to my heartbeat. ♪♫

The music owns me and my feet begin to dance.
Looking down, my legs are slim and brown again
and my old cherry red Docs are on my feet,
feet than can skank without getting tired
and I'm wearing the little dress, the one I love,
that hasn't fitting me in years. ♪♫

With a wave of bliss, I realise
this is the best night of my life.
This club never closes,
the bar never stops serving
and the songs never end. ♪♫

I died last night
and I've been given the golden ticket.
So when you look up at that star,
don't you be worrying about me
because this is where I'm happy,
dancing to the music and drinking at the bar. ♪♫

It's where I'll be waiting for you, to get you one in…

Just Wait

Our life paths twist
And our life paths turn
And we never learn
That a walk in the dark
Is a temporary thing
That around the corner
Across the next hill
The sun is shining
And blackbirds sing
Our feet may stumble
We may feel humble
But the light waits to
Illuminate everything

The Bells

In Kinver Churchyard,
Bells vibrate, shake out
Last fingers of the sun,
Rumble down the echo,
Awaking bats
And swarms of gnats.
Clouds of three dimensions
Push angry grey to front
While, behind,
Tinged in tired light,
Pale peach
Flings petals
To the dying singe
To bid me goodnight,
Tolling out my own mortality
And far beyond
Infinity
And my divinity.

The Here and Now

I look at you and wonder how
To pin this happy here and now
Down to the floor and lock the door
And keep you here forever more.

Stop changing now, stop aging now,
For I cannot imagine how
This world will spin without you in,
For you have been my everything.

But let's not dwell on things so glum
Or what will be in years to come,
We can smile, so laugh awhile,
Turn life's allegro to a strum.

YOU ARE THE POET

When we open a book and glance at the page
We already know the end is made,
Pre-written, pre-destined, each character set,
Each plot-turn and twist already laid.

There may be endings that give us a shock
Or times we will guess how things pan out
But we know the story is already told,
However much we rail and shout.

But there is one story that no one knows,
One ending not set in stone,
Conspiracy, complicity all unknown
Who fails, who wins, who ends alone.

So open your book and write on the page.
Who cries, who tries, who dies, who lies?
Let your stories flow from your pen,
The ending is all yours; only yours to decide.

You are the writer, victim or fighter,
Choose between gladness or strife.
Complete your story, death or glory,
You! Yes you, the poet of your life.

Part Three

- ♀ -

Turning Circles

To Matt, because
circles have no beginning or end

My Guitar Man

When I am lonely, I think of you
On a hill, in a forest, beneath Spring blue
Amid one hundred hues of green
Sat cross-legged in old ripped jeans

We were celebrating. Three years of dating
Learning and growing, together creating
We carried up bread and cheese and wine
Along the brook, beneath the pine

We climbed up to our secret spot
A place that time and space forgot
And in the bracken and trees among
You played your guitar and sang me a song

You had written it, scripted it, solely for me
Hidden, in secret, so I could not see
With a self-conscious look upon your face
You sang just for me, in that wild place

Your long hair gleamed in the fading light
Our only disturbance, a bird in flight
And in that moment, my heart burst
My love, my life, my last, my first

Your Lottie xxx
Magical Order of the DragonSnake

‖BOUNDARIES‖

My grandmother used to say,
Your soul is all you have,
The rest of you is nothing,
Just atoms from a long-forgotten star,
It's not who you are.

So you keep good boundaries, girl,
Around the garden of your soul
Because the winds of life, they will howl around it
And the wolves of life, they will prowl around it,
Looking for a weak spot before tearing you apart.

Boundaries mean knowing when to say *no*.
Boundaries mean knowing when to put *yourself* first.
Boundaries mean knowing when to *walk away*.
So when a man makes you cry,
When he looks you in the eyes and he lies,
When his hand is so big he has to curl it in a fist,
Then it's time to walk away.

If, after years of dating, you don't feature in his future,
You will never feature.
If you cook for him each day but the food bill is not his business,
He will never share the bills.
If he sneaks off to screw other women
Then you are the one who is screwed.

If this happens, rest assured
The posts of your boundaries have worked themselves loose
And the seeds that invade will grow into weeds
And smother the petals of the girl you once were.

When a man you have loved for years, tells you
He can't commit to you
But neither can he let you go,
He has dropped you into the abyss.

And the months pass and you are still feeding him,
A hundred showers but the gas bill is not his problem,
And you don't know how it got this way,

And you hate yourself, berate yourself,
And you beat yourself up...
Beat, beat, your heart feels beaten.

When my grandmother was alive,
Her wisdoms hung like fruits from the tree,
And although the fruit is rotten
It is not forgotten
For the juices drip into my mind.
I remember her words,
Your soul is all you have,
The rest of you is nothing,
Just dust from a distant star,
It's not who you are.

So, pick up a mallet,
However heavy, however much it weighs you down
And bang each post back into the earth of yourself.
Each swing will crash your hopes and dreams;
Each swing will break your heart
And it will bleed, mourning for the years
But you will be intact
And your garden will flourish.

With a mallet on your shoulder
And a piece of rotten fruit clasped inside your hand,
You wade down that stream and into your future.
Your soul is all you have,
Respect it,
Because in the end,
There is only you to protect it.
So you keep good boundaries, girl,
And you know when to walk away.

Done With Dating Sites

Bipolar, biracial, bisexual,
50-something, left-Libertarian witch
Seeks long-term relationship
With like-minded alien.
Looks not important
Although...
Not a fan of the hipster-lizard-look
But I like a nice tentacle. *(Laughing emoji)*
Must have own moral compass
To navigate the universe
And a liking for mead.
Cosy nights in with bondage rope
And the occasional blood ritual.
Mature enough to manage my psychosis
And hold me on the edge of the planet -
And take it in good humour
Because I take it ALL in good humour...
(Winking emoji)
If you are Mr or Miss Perfect,
Take me for a spin
On the back of your spaceship.
All messages replied to in basic binary
Or Egyptian hieroglyphics
But if you can write in Klingon,
Expect to get laid on our first date.
Sadly, by the time this reaches you
I'll have been dead for light years,
So just swipe past my profile.
(Sad emoji)
(Sad emoji)

Flowers

Cheap flowers from the garage,
given with such love.
We laugh at the gaudiness,
the limp one, hanging head,
one carnation, too big, too pink
to blend in with the rest.
I sit them in the window
and the sun is so intense
the petals singe.
Oh, heat!
The wailing, thrashing heat
of new-love summer.
'I have no car, but I
will walk eight miles,' you say,
'from my house up to yours.
Make love', you say,
'right here, right now,
on the carpet.'

An ebbing sun shuts summer down
and you are wearied
by the sinking light. I need
my space, you say. When
I get time off work,
we'll find a way to
recreate the past.
I dream I find your flowers

rotting in the window.
Oh, dead!
Funny, heartfelt flowers.
How did I forget?
Petals parched, leaves
Shriveled, husks dry,
dry as my body.
I touch the cheek of a rose-head,
It crumbles, rains dust,
dust on the carpet.

Fucking Man
(or How Many Times Can I Say "Fuck" in a Poem?)

You made me fucking sad, Man.
Yes, you, Man, you made me cry.
There were many reasons why
but we know the main ones, don't we?
Ears pricked, have they?
There you go, now you know,
this one's about YOU.

How differently you view the past.
Man, that warped view lasts
because snakes and slugs and thugs
have beautiful abilities
to turn themselves into the victim.
How the fuck did YOU become the victim?

Your whiney voice drones on
about how hard it is for YOU.
Man, you broke my heart,
shattered it, then spattered it
like a damaged back,
like a bolted door,
like the blood of a foetus.
What? Gone too far?
Yeah, you know who you fucking are.

To be fair, Man, you're one of a number.
No one special, just A or B or C or fucking Z.
In my head, I wait for an apology,
A long, overdue apology
That never fucking comes.
"I'm sorry. I treated you bad. It makes me sad."

And STOP the conversation...///
Don't say "BUT".
Don't say YOU, Man, are the one who got hurt.
I fucking hate you when you do that.

You don't know how much I fucking hate you.
You don't know how much I fucking loved you.
In case you can't tell, I'm frankly still fucking angry.

Call yourself a Man, Man?
Man, you're not a Man, Man.

Left at the Altar

The dream is old and also new,
I borrow love; it makes me blue.
My dress is trailing through the dirt,
My bridal shoes, they hurt.
A hollow toast, like love that never grew.

I hold dead flowers within my hands
And broken hearts and broken plans.
My bridal car, it broke,
Stopped dead in clouds of smoke,
It clatters strings of baked bean cans

And empty bottles of champagne
I drink alone through nights of pain.
I'm stuck behind my veil,
My hopes have all gone stale.
I'm at the bus-stop in the rain.

LOSS

Waking this morning, I'm missing an arm
and a leg, and a piece of my soul.
Half of my life, in the night, fell inside
the cavernous, ravenous hole
left in the mattress your side of the bed.
Now my heart is as hollow inside
and empty as a cockle shell
washed up by the tears of the tide.

L♥ve

The only certainty of love, is pain.
Unrequited pain; goodbye insane pain;
Disappointed, hopes-dashed pain;
Weary run-its-course pain
Or dreary try-and-force pain;
The fiery angst of not-yet pain
And the deadly drip of betrayal.

And yet, I meet your lips and
Mine will not stop trembling,
For pain is not enough to kill this passion
And I will never learn.

OUR LAST DANCE

Do you remember our last dance
 As we gracefully circled the face of time,
 Unaware of the midnight advance
 Or the ink drying at the end of our rhyme?

We were up on the stage of the future,
 Wanting the music to last and last,
 Stealing more time like a looter,
 Our intricate steps tracing the past.

The audience clapped us and cheered,
 Willing us to remember the steps
 But soon, the music disappeared
 And it all became far too complex

In the confusion, we stumbled,
 You stepped on the hem of my delicate gown
 And our lifetime performance crumbled
 As the final curtain came down.

Packed up Summer

A lot packed up and left this summer.
We never made it to Carefree, did we?
Like years ago, when you were me
And I was you and we were two,
We feared no hourglass dripping sand,
When hand in hand, we laughed.

I lost an old friend; we both lost a new.
We were shocked by our grieving, weren't we?
They focussed it, and for no fee
They took it from us, happily,
Though it was not about passed souls.
Our other ghouls, they laughed.

Don't laugh at the hourglass any more,
We won't even look at it, sweet pea.
Our hands apart, our final dart
Has pierced the shroud, and yet, too proud
To voice our failings, we'll stay on.
Til winter's white, we'll laugh.

A lot packed up and left this summer,
We never quite reached True Love, did we?
I've noticed now that I am me
And you are you, we are not two.
Hope, trust, lust, love...
A lot packed up and left this summer.

It will be awhile before we laugh again.

Tartan Shorts

How many socks? I ask,
And shall I pack your tartan shorts?
There's a tear in the turn-up
But they've been on every beach
Since nineteen ninety-two.

You shrug. Which shorts?

Your holiday shorts,
Your lucky shorts,
Your slot-machine
Chase-me-down-the-pier
Throw-me-in-the-surf shorts.

No, I don't recall.

Your tartan shorts,
Your hand-in-hand-beach-walk shorts,
Your too-many-beers-serious-talk shorts,
Your kneeling-in-the sand-ring-in-hand shorts,
Your shorts.

I don't know which shorts you're referring to.

Your cliff-walk shorts,
Your scrambling-rocks shorts,
Your winning-the-drinking-game
Kissing-in-the-rain
Saying-I-love-you shorts.

I don't care, I have to send an email.

Upstairs, I sense you downstairs...

Messaging HER.

I cram in pants and jeans
And shoes and shirts
There's room on top for books
Your glasses and your
Heartburn tablets

I drag your case downstairs
Bump, bump down each step
Open the door and throw it in the road
What the hell? You ask.

I hold the door as you leave
Put the shorts in your hands
And say...

These are the fucking shorts I'm referring to.

a moment

I lie behind you,

your hair across the pillow,

light, white like a halo,

a luminous pool in the darkened room

and I wish, how I wish I were an artist.

I would trace the curve of your back,

capture the white shoulder

as it slides into the sheet,

and with pastels as soft as your skin,

shade in your nightlight

as it illuminates the small hand

lying on the pillow.

but I have no skill,

only hopeless, helpless, heartless words,

so instead, I tenderly kiss your head,

find my scattered clothes

and steal from the room,

knowing the image will die

the moment I leave your house.

Part Four

- ♀ -

Hint of Humour

To Beth and James B,
the happiest people I know

Better late than never

(For Beth & James B)

Come on, hurry up. You're late.
What time do you call this?
Where were you in those weeks,
those months, those years?
I didn't even know you.
How did I not know you?
To think there was a time we
sat at the same table and did not speak.
I didn't know your names.
James thought I didn't like him,
I thought he didn't like me,
Now we're like family.
How weird is that?
And Beth appeared from nowhere
And we didn't let her go.
So, better late than never,
the last to arrive,
the first to make me smile.
James of 'The Laugh' and
Beth of the 'Wonderlust',
So glad you finally showed up,
Because I always feel happy
When you are around.

Fifty Shades of Menopause

I used to be carefree, used to be young,
There was wine to be drunk and songs to be sung,
The original rebel without a cause
Until I was struck by the menopause.

The first signs came with aches and pains
And a kind of fogginess in me brains.
When I call me partner from upstairs,
I go through at least seven names…

Rosie, George, no, David, Matt,
Let the potatoes in and boil the cat,
And to his annoyance and my lasting shame
I keep calling him by me ex-husband's name.

I'm constantly dyeing the roots of me hair
And I've started to groan when I stand from me chair.
I've found that I now can't drive in the dark
And I've lost the ability to parallel park.

I'm a little bit moody, it has to be said,
Me road rage has become something to dread.
I used to moan when I was having sex
But I moan more now when I can't find me specs.

Painting me toe nails makes me hips feel crippled
So I just tie the brush to the end of me nipples
And I'm going to be honest, I won't tell a lie,
Everything's gone a little bit dry,

Except when me body sweats so much
I nearly drown in me own hot flush.
But finally, salvation come to me
And sent me the angel of HRT.

The First Time

Do you remember your first time?
I know you do. We all remember our first time.
I would like to tell you that my first time
Took place in a woodland glade
With my unicorn tethered to a tree
Or a four-poster bed strung with fairy lights
Or even a tent at Glastonbury
But no, this momentous event took place
on the hideous green 70s-patterned carpet
In front of a 3-bar electric fire
When my mum popped to Woolworths
And Timmy, the stinky Yorkshire Terrier, licked my toes
I was nervous, because in those days
I thought a boner was actually made of bone
And as I couldn't yet insert a tampon
I had no idea how I would accommodate
Something akin to a leg of lamb
But I took courage, I was well informed
I had read the sex tips in Jackie Magazine
But when I saw this monstrous, humungous, uncircumcised
Thirteen-year old penis
I thought I may have been reading the wrong magazines
That lead-up kiss, that first trembling fumble
Eyes all aglow, hair all a-tumble
We didn't know what we were doing
But in the holy words of the Bay City Rollers
When the sun comes shining through, we'll know what to do
He didn't find the clitoris
But in his defence, I didn't know I had one
And the lad was some kind of stud, I reckon
He lasted at least a full 90 seconds
But I have to say, it was all an anti-climax
(Maybe because I didn't know what climax meant)

And afterwards, we lay on the hideous carpet
A little kiss, and a little sigh
Knowing we must not fall asleep
Because mom was coming back to make shepherd's pie
But my eyes began to droop, and I drifted off
And slept like a baby
When I woke up, I was 55 years old
And the intervening years have been nothing but a dream
During which sex got a lot, lot better
And post-thirteen cocks made me much, much wetter
And I have seen sex in its warped entirety
Loving sex, angry sex, S&M sex, and guilty sex
Some stands out, and some was rotten
But face it, that first time
Is printed in indelible ink
And is never, ever forgotten

One Hundred Ways to Write A Poem

One hundred ways
To set down scrabbled tiles of thought
Or throw the cards into the air,
The slippery, glittery, witchery of words.
A hundred ways to gracefully slip
Some fifty thousand adjectives
And too many crazily, lazily, hazily adverbs
Into a carefully crafted stanza.

Some write in rhyme
Like the quick beat of time
But, don't force it
Like a drip from a faucet
Because we don't say faucet in the UK.
And metre is important,
Isn't it?

So pick up your pen
Open your laptop
Hone your ideas
And fling them at us.
We'll catch them, I promise.
We want to see songs
Litter the page
Like a music score.
They can never be 'wrong'
You're just humming a song.

It good to know the rules
But rules can be broken
Or never learned
And if someone's hung up on them
They've missed the point,
The lyrics were misheard

And they will forever sing the wrong words.

Poetry is like...
Thought
in motion,
A snapshot of frozen life-pixels,
A tableaux in words,
It's art.
So, go on, you purists -
Tear me apart.

The Counsellor

Let me tell you about my day.
Today has been a bad day, a sad day,
I need to get it off my chest. Oh, chest, I think there's a lump in
this breast,
Cop a feel, or does that transcend professional boundaries?

You see, I'm afraid of getting old with no one to hold,
My relationships have been like slaughter, can't keep my head
above the water
Or is it me? I think I may have serious commitment issues.

Last night, I thought I'd had a stroke, it's not a joke.
My head went numb, there was tingling in my thumbs,
Do you think I'm a hypochondriac?

And I'm worried about my pension. I need a life extension
Of at least fifty years, I've wasted so much time and tears
On poor choices.

I know what you'll tell me. I'm a fifty year old divorcee.
I should really start to plan my future, stop living in a stupor
Before I die in bed and am eaten by my cat.

I know how it works, there are no quick perks, so I'll keep
circling the same shit because I'm not quite getting it
But plan B is the lottery.

Oh, quick! I have to put my thoughts away. It's time for Mrs.
Grey.
The door opens and in she sways. Ahh, looks like she's having a
bad day.
I say, "Hello, Mrs. Grey. How are things with you today?"

As I fix a reassuring look upon my face.

Dry January

The first of January is going to be
A brand new start and a healthy me
So the first thing to go, must be the beers,
They're bringing me poor old liver to tears.
The whole of January is going to be dry,
(Hang on, I'll just wipe a tear from me eye).
So off I go, round the shops in a blur
To stock up on cranberry and some filth called Shloer
I lock up the wine, with a bit of a twinge
And there it will wait for the February binge.
I fall out with tequila, boot out Jack,
Replaced with herb tea in a full-scale attack.
By the third of January, I'm feeling quite smug,
All thoughts of failure cast off with a shrug,
But it's bloody cold, so it's a kind of self-slaughter
To sit in a pub with a Perrier water.
And as you lot get stuck into wine and to song
I suddenly wonder if I've got this all wrong.
January, the worst month of the year,
Dark mornings, no sun, with nothing to cheer.
I'm beginning to think I may have fucked-up
By announcing me intentions on bloody facebook.
But I soldier on for another few days,
Only three weeks 'til a glass I can raise.
By the tenth of January, I'm feeling quite blue
I miss getting pissed with me Katie's crew.
On the twelfth, I crack, develop a twitch
Start calling dry January a *fucking bitch*.
So, I'd rather spend time with a girl called Failure
And tonight, I intend to fucking nail her.
Cheers!

Some Woman in Purple Trousers told me I Should Practice Gratefulness for being Menopausal

Dear Divine Consciousness
I am truly grateful that I have reached menopause and I'm still here
The fact that I haven't died of cirrhosis
Or a drug overdose
Is living proof of your miracles
I am grateful for my food, my shelter
That my children are healthy
For my friends and family
And all that are gathered here tonight
However, whilst I hesitate to question your infinite wisdom
While the channels of communication are open
And the pen is in my hand
I have a few questions
Things I am struggling with
After decades of pleasurable moistness
I fail to see the cosmic significance of a dry vajayjay
I have endured the monthly bleeds, the thrush infections
And the smear tests in the spirit of my goddess fertility
So it seems a bit rich that now the kids are out the house
And I can have sex at the drop of a hat
I need more lubrication than a C-plate Morris Minor
On the same subject, I'm unclear, oh great one, how my consciousness is elevated
By peeing when I sneeze and farting when I tie my laces
Oh, Creator, divine architect of the universe
Help me understand why I've lost the ability to remember
More than two things at once
Including where I parked my car
And sometimes my children's names

And whilst I appreciate the expended calories
Of running upstairs, why make me do it three times
Before I remember what I went for?
I am grateful for the confidence that age brings to the
bedroom
I am not afraid to ask for what I want
But when I get my legs over my head,
I am unable to walk for three solid days
And if I did swing from a chandelier
I'm pretty sure I would dislocate both shoulders
I don't mind the crows feet, the greying hair
Or leaving my left indicator on for two and a half hours
But why, oh why, oh magnificent one
Do my knees sound like bubble wrap when I walk downstairs
And I won't even mention body hair
When I was young I wanted big boobs
But now the fucking things won't stop growing
And their sense of direction is all wrong
My bras resemble the wire netting
That holds together the Forth bridge
And finally, oh designer of the cosmos
Answer me one last question, if you can
Am I right in thinking you're a bloody man?

Part Five

- ♀ -

LGBTQ+ Pride

To Jamie and James L,
making gay great again

My Husband

(For James L)

We joke that we'll get married
(Some people think we already are)
Of course, sadly, that won't happen
Not least because I'm in love with your friend
And you are massively gay
But in the absence of legal wedding vows
I have this to say:

I call upon these persons here present, to witness that you, James
Lowe, are a beautiful soul.

I promise to respect you; support you through difficult times; rejoice
with you through happy times; be loyal to you always; and above all,
love you as my 'husband' and friend.

I promise to drink with you and make you miss your bus; text to make
sure you're home, because I *always* forget; tell you the latest gossip, as
long as you return the favour; and sit outside with you, even though
I've quit smoking.

In the future, I promise to cry at your wedding (preferably in
happiness), to babysit your children, turn up pissed to your parties and
love you 'til death do us part.

Gaymen

JAMIE

There are times when sentences, discipline, structure or sense, do not apply. There is only a splat. Anyone who knows the lovely Jamie, will understand exactly what I'm talking about.

BumboySaphire
SpecialShots heels
GAY performance.
LipSync hair late Lashes
makeup wig
PRIDE dye nails friend
drag DIANA tequila
hangover pissed
LeopardPrint
Jamie

Are You Straight or Are You Gay?

Why are you so interested in my sexuality?
It's not as if I'm into snuff or kids or bestiality
And yet, you're still determined to tag me with a label.
Come on, you say, let's talk it out,
Let's get it on the table.
Are you straight or are you gay?
I need to tell your Aunty May.
Have you heard what the neighbours say?
First, you have that boy called Jay
And now, it seems, you're into Faye.

Why don't you just make your mind up?
Don't keep sitting on the fence,
It's playing havoc with our nerves
All this guessing and suspense.
If you want to be a *"lesbian"*
Well, that's alright with us,
Even Grandma understands that,
She saw one once, on the bus.
But, are you straight or are you gay?
Make a choice, either way,
Don't keep changing every day,
What's your father going to say?
It's us, you know who have to pay.

And I reply...look, I'm not a bloody pigeon
You can just stick in a box,
I have two legs, two eyes, a heart,
I like music and writing,
I like pre-Raphaelite art.
Does it matter who I fuck?
For me, this way is better,
Man or woman, gay straight or trans,
It just depends who makes me WETTER.

Frank

His name was Frank,
From the corner of our street,
His eyes were...blank,
He seemed a bit depressed, downbeat,
Quite sad, I think.
Although polite, I never saw him smile,
Pushed to the brink,
Never accepted,
Sent into teenage exile.

Fast forward, then:
A night spent drinking,
dancing on the floor,
The same night that a woman entered,
All eyes on the door.
A stunning girl, more beautiful
Than I had ever seen,
All ringlet curls
Against a dress of darkest green.

She walked with poise
Across the floor,
And all eyes followed her,
All the boys became tongue-tied and
Tried to dance with her.
She caught my eye and my heart smiled
and silently I blessed her.
How very dry that only I
Knew Frank was now Franchesca.

Some of my best friends are gay

Live and let live, that's what I say,
some of MY BEST FRIENDS are gay.
Do whatever floats your boat,
just don't ram it down my throat.

See, I don't want to be a churl,
but man with man and girl on girl
goes against the NATURAL ORDER,
all confusion and disorder.

Although I keep an open mind...
I'm just concerned about mankind.
The nuclear family's threatened here,
by you DECIDING to be queer.

I know I'll be hated for having a voice,
but think about your LIFESTYLE CHOICE.
I expect I'll be criticised terribly
for even suggesting conversion therapy.

But I'm really NOT HOMOPHOBIC,
all I'm doing is having a say.
Live and let live, that's my motto.
Hey, some of my best friends are gay.

Stolen Pride

Gay Pride is in its 48th year
And I'm really happy to be here,
But let's just remember what's happening in Chechnya.

We *should* feel pride that we no longer hide.
We're mainstream now, we're bona fide.
Enjoy the ride.

But let's not develop amnesia
About events in Indonesia.

Hey, you're justified to feel gratified,
That we're no longer outcasts,
And with the turn of that tide
Our rights aren't denied.

But remember Sudan, Iran and Afghanistan,
Qatar and Pakistan.

In thirteen countries
Love as natural as drawing breath
Is punishable by death.

And let's just be clear, even here,
In a world that Trump is left to steer
Our freedoms may become unsteady
And we *have* to be ready.

There are some who want to smash us,
Those goddam bible bashers,
But so far, we're winning the fight,
We're doing alright.

But our brothers and sisters
Reside where it's suicide.
So many beaten, so many died.

They're identified, tried,
Strict laws applied,
People terrified.
And you know how it ends…
Fucking genocide.

There's one way this can be classified,
It's sexual apartheid.

And for what?
For love?

So, from all of us here
To all those, there,
To people living in fear and despair,
We raise our flag to you,

Because your freedoms are *way* overdue.

Middle of the Spectrum

I used to wish I had a penis
So I could fuck Denise Andelenis,
She went to my school and man, she was hot.
So, what?
Should I start jumping in teenage confusion
To some kind of conclusion?
Was there a man trapped in here?
Umm, I did like bikes and beer
But then, make-up and heels
Had their appeal.
Oh, crap! Does that mean
Inside me, there's a drag queen?
A drag queen inside me?
(That's pretty unlikely)
But then, I met Hugh. Phew!
He made me feel like a woman
And a natural one, it has to be said.
I didn't want a penis
When I rolled with him around the bed.
But a few months down the line
I was rolling round with Caroline,
It was a very confusing time.
Sometimes I felt like a woman,
Sometimes I felt like a man,
But most of the time, I felt in between,
I didn't belong to either team
Because back in the day, I have to say,

When I identified as Bi,
I was excluded with impunity
From the straight **and** the gay community.
And anyway, Bi didn't explain me
Because Bi, in Latin, means two,
But there's more than two...
There's me and there's you
And there's you and there's you and there's you.
(Oh, hello! Wink. And you!)
We all perch on the spectrum,
Some this end, some that end,
And some just in the reflection
Of who we want to be.
Do you see?
And I'm not sure how,
But I'm fashionable now
And finally, I'm proud to be non-binary.
Oh, and I didn't need a penis
To fuck Denise Andelenis.

The Name's Lottie

It's a strange thing, a name.
It takes on an energy all of its own.
My name is Charlotte, or Lottie or Charlie,
At least, that's what everyone called me at home.

But outside of home, my name was changed,
It had a different destiny.
What was I called? Well, the names ranged
And became my new identity.

Lottie the Lezzer
Button Flicker, Clit Licker
And those who thought I was just in a *phase,*
Pussy Bumper, Rug Muncher
And Gillette Blade, 'cus I cut both ways.

Attention Seeker, Curtain Tweaker,
Nipple Sucker, Greedy Fucker
Or just that confused bird
Who sometimes stirred the bean curd.

Okay, it was the eighties
And no one was meant to be Bi.
Some folk took it as offence
They couldn't push me off the fence
And oh, Lord, did they try.

But that was then, and this is now,
I don't know how we got here,
But I have to say, it feels okay,
So I'll take the L and the B and the Queer.

Oh, and the name's **LOTTIE** by the way
And I'm off to have a beer.

Part Six

- ♀ -

Political Outrage

To Cam, because
one day, you'll change the world

Kameron

Mental'nyy
Nasha blondinka detka

Nash Kameron

I suspect google translate let me down and this makes no
sense. Like your memes.

Austerity Vulgarity

A **young man** has died, no cash for the meter
As his insulin warms in the fridge.
An **old man** has died, would not use his heater
And a **mother's** thrown herself from a bridge.
A **woman** attends her young child's funeral
And has her benefits stopped.
600,000 with not enough food
Use **food banks** instead of the shops.
A terminal man declared **fit for work**
Dies the first day on the job.
A **homeless** man has his tent torn down
And police encourage the mob.
A quadriplegic is asked to show proof
That he can't reach the loo on his own
And a brain-cancer **patient** with four weeks to live
Has to prove that her tumour has grown.
20,000 **police** off the beat, our **NHS** in decline,
400,000 **kids** now live below the poverty line.
One hundred and thirty four percent
Is the rise in sleeping rough
And two-income working people
Struggle to earn enough.
Austerity, the price we pay, right?
To bring down the national debt
So why, after three elections
Are we still in deficit?
Yet money is found to **bomb** and **kill**
In countries that pose no threat.
This is the biggest transfer of wealth
From the **poor** to the rich, and yet
People keep voting the Tories back.
Call me simple, I don't understand that.

One day, in the future, when your grandchildren ask
On which side did you stand today,
Will you be able to look in their eyes?
What will **you** be able to say?

Dear Daily Mail

Criminalise all the homeless!
They clutter up the pavement,
Tucked up in dirty sleeping bags
In drug induced enslavement.
When I've hit all the Christmas sales
I need lunch and cocktails,
Not some stinking homeless man
With blackened, dirty nails.

Lock up all the drug addicts!
They're a danger to society,
Responsible for every crime
With no sense of propriety.
Why should my tax pay for rehab
Diverting cash away?
The amount of beer and fags I smoke,
I'll need that back some day.

Send back all the foreigners!
Protect the British way of life,
Punch ups after fourteen pints
And home to beat the wife.
You know what I'm talking about,
Pandering to other cultures,
Whilst they take our jobs and welfare
Like fucking hungry vultures.

Bring down all the feminists!
We're in a right old fix,
Can't even get a shirt ironed
Or a meal on the table at six.
Those feminazis ruined it all

By being way too pushy,
It's time to take our power back boys
And grab 'em by the pussy.

And finally, castrate the gays!
To call them men is libel,
It goes against our nature
And the teachings of the bible.
Getting married, having kids,
That's not how I was taught.
No son of mine will be a pansy,
I'd knock him out if he was caught.

I know your readers feel the same
And so do you, it's clear,
It's printed in your pages here,
The hatred and the fear.
We turn to you for British values
And you corroborate,
A newspaper of distinction
That I must congratulate.

Yours truly
Dickhead

Dear Syrian Refugee

I write to put my case forward
I hope you understand
You should not have headed shoreward
You should have stayed on land

When Nazi jackboots threatened us
We didn't show this fear
We did what needed to be done
Course, the fighting wasn't here

You should have stayed and fought for it
That dirty desert, rough
Joining one side or the other
Er, not clear on all that stuff

There seems to be a bunch of you
Assad, rebels, ISIS too,
You should get your house in order
Work out who is who

We'd be more accommodating
If we weren't so full
Exact same problem that we had
Before the Jewish cull

The other problem here, you see
The threat to our small nation
We know your hidden agenda

Is Muslim domination

And we've been told by our proud press
With honesty and candour
You're whipped into a frenzy
By religious propaganda

And even if this all could be
Put one side a moment
We know you're harbouring terrorists
For which there's no atonement

So, quite a big mistake, I think
There's no life here of leisure
I hope you get it sorted though
I don't like all this pressure

Hope

What happens to a person
when they see the world as it really is?
How do they live
when the sky is not blue and the grass is not green
and everything they've ever seen is overturned,
dead and burned?

What happens to a person
when they thought they stood on the side of truth?
A wasted youth,
when the truth was a lie,
distorted misery
became a dead reality, a mystery,
our history.

So when the good guys became the bad guys
and the bad became the good,
I no longer knew where I stood.
Farewell Iraq and Libya,
try to hold on Syria
but to those in Iran,
look to Afghanistan,
for our world has become one endless Vietnam.

What happens to a person
when she's left alone to prop up the truth?
Our burning roof,
with her feet in the mud,

tired shoulders,
her arms will break beneath boulders that smoulder,
this stakeholder.

What happens to a person
when everything she was taught in school
means nothing, nothing at all?
While we flail around in greed and lies,
the civilised,
but someone dies, they always die.
there's oil to buy.

So when the good guys became the bad guys
and the bad became the good,
I no longer knew where I stood.
Farewell Iraq and Libya,
try to hold on Syria
but to those in Iran,
look to Afghanistan,
for our world has become one endless Vietnam.

Hush

Hush, my little dolly,
There is no need to scream,
The soldiers, they have promised
To bring us pink ice-cream.
They told me that the next bomb
is filled with strawberry jelly,
So we can stuff it down
Inside our hungry little bellies.
And Daddy's only playing
At lying in the road
And Mummy was so hot,
The soldiers helped take off her clothes.
But we have to get our sister now,
I hear her baby cries.
No, don't look in the pram, my dear,
I'll cover up your eyes.
So hush, my little dolly,
There is no need to scream,
We'll wake up in the morning
And today will be a dream.

Lifted

᠙᠙᠙᠙᠙᠙᠙᠙᠙᠙᠙᠙᠙᠙᠙᠙᠙

I had a dream last night
That each person upon the earth
Laid down their ego
And their greed
And their envy
And desire for wealth
And one hundred avoidance techniques
That prevent us seeing the world
And we opened our hearts
And compassion spewed forth.

It lit up dark places, empty people,
Fed them, housed them, loved them,
Illuminating
The children
On rubbish tips
And the rough sleepers
And the bombed cities across the world
And right into our governments.
There was no need for war,
Indeed, when we looked back...

We could hardly believe
How far we had fallen.

Monday Revolution

I wake in the dark,
no birds, I'm awake before the bloody birds.
I shiver at the basin, blind eyes blinking...
We're slaves! All of us, slaves.
There are resources on this planet
to feed and house and educate us all.
We should not have to stand
on a platform in the rain
heading into forty hours of dullness
down the tracks of serfdom.
There has to be a better way
and today is the day to work it out.
A woman rams a pushchair in my leg
and I scream at the pain,
the sun is not yet up
my feet are already wet.
This is it! My Monday Revolution.
On the tedious train
I'll think of the solution
...when I've read this free newspaper
and had a hot coffee,
then I'll be ready for anarchy.
But as I walk from the station
the birds are singing
and in the office, a stack of emails
await my attention
and anarchy will have to wait
until next Monday morning.

Red Heart

My forefathers worked in the cotton fields
Singing through their desperate days
I grew up in a small, white town
So different in every way
When I look up to the skies above
I hear their voices sing
On desperate days, I take their strength
And let salvation in

Because I'm white on the outside
But black on the inside
Like an apple sliced apart
White on the outside
Black on the inside
But everybody has a red heart

When I think of their mournful lives
Tears roll down my face
Broken backs and wills of steel
And songs so full of grace
Deep inside my two-tone soul
I try to understand
How a proud and ancient race
Were taken from their lands

Because I'm white on the outside
But black on the inside
Like an apple sliced apart

White on the outside
Black on the inside
But everybody has a red heart

My words lead to where they led
Everybody bleeds red
And everybody has a red heart.

Somewhere Out There

Somewhere out there is a grave,
A grave beneath the sea,
A silent, stunted, watery space
Where he sleeps safe and free.

My beautiful Amira,
For days you walked with me,
Growing palely silent, drawn,
Your eyes a hollow plea.

I could hardly look at you, my love,
You thought compassion gone,
But I knew you could rest as soon as
We had boarded on.

I longed for you in clean sheets,
Brown curls spread over them
With Ali purring at your feet
And sloppy licks from Gem.

On the boat now, tossed and full,
I sensed your pains had started,
Soon you screamed in walls of waves
That crashed and then departed.

I spread you on the slick, wet deck
You writhed in agony,
I prayed to Allah, tenfold,
Don't take them both from me.

I timed his life in bursts of spray,
And hidden by the crowd,

You did not see me use, my love,
A bin bag for his shroud.

Weights from tins of fava beans,
I kissed his blood-stained head
And tossed him in the steely sea,
Forever now his bed.

He floated there, a symbol,
I watched him slowly sink,
The crime scene of humanity,
I see between each blink.

OH BROTHER

Oh, Brother,
I held a torch for you,
and watched you wrestle with the world.
Our mother taught me how to sew
And I stitched wings for you and watched you soar.
But you made flags and went to war,
We should not do this anymore.
You made flags and went to war,
I cannot do this anymore.

You can walk alone
Til there's no place left to hide
Or you can take my hand
And have me walking by your side.
You can walk alone
Til the last green tree has died
Or you can take my hand
And we'll start building side by side.

Oh, Brother,
Without my shadow side,
Your light cannot provide the shade.
Our mother bled and so do I
So we could love the earth as one.
But a daughter does not match a son
For we care not who lost or won,
A daughter does not match a son
I do not care who lost or won.

You can walk alone
Til there's no place left to hide
Or you can take my hand
And have me walking by your side.
You can walk alone
Til the last green tree has died
Or you can take my hand
And we'll start building side by side.

You can take our hands
And together we'll survive.

The Future Could Be Bright and Not Orange
(Tweet, tweet. Tweet, tweet.)

I don't think any of us thought it could happen,
That a chump like Trump with a nuclear strap-on,
A caricature, an orange louse,
Would actually sit in the bloody White House.

Leader of the free western world,
How quickly his end-games began to unfurl.
He soon got into the steady rhythm
Of taking America back to fascism.

With hands like a puppet and a face like a ham,
He's calling for war on the whole of Islam.
Oh, and Mexicans and of course, North Korea,
And sending more troops to stir up Crimea.

He's lied about Syria, fucked with Iran,
Silently returning his troops to Afghan,
Denies climate change, the silly great lemon,
But he doesn't give a shit about Yemen.

He's pulled the rug from under the poor,
Ditched Obama-care, shown it the door
And if that's not enough, he has to keep trimming,
By messing with contraception for women.

Now I don't believe in a violent outcome
But when a dangerous man has the world under thumb,
I'm only thinking what you want to shout…
It's about bloody time someone took that cunt out.

(I meant 'out' as in out for dinner, Mr FBI-man)

Part Seven

- ♀ -

Random Stuff

For Jess, Harry, Mary, Jess Silk, Nathan, Patrick, Ian, Paul, Laura, Simon, Sally and all my Katie's partners in crime. Love you.

And tequila. I love you too.

Katie Fitzgerald's

I've spent a lot of my life in pubs,
Drinking away my monthly wage,
I thought it was something I'd leave behind
But it seems I'm incapable of learning with age.
Dry Januaries come
And dry Januaries go
And I never get to the end
Because come nine, it all feels wrong
And I want to be out with my friends.
And then I found Katie's, for good or for bad,
For times when I'm happy,
For times when I'm sad.
And it doesn't matter how often I swore
That I'd never darken the bloody door,
Most nights of the week, I'm out on that deck
And next day, turn up to work like a wreck.
I don't know why this pub pulls me in,
Is it Trina's kiss, is it Eddy's grin?
Or is it because of the social leaning,
We're all a bit left, if you take my meaning.
It could be the music, we all like a tune
Or because I know most folk in the room.
I've had some dark moments in this pub,
Losing a friend that everyone loved,
Losing the vote to the other side
And I was here the night my mother died.
But they're not the memories I keep in my heart
On mornings I struggle to work in the dark.
The overriding memories of here
Are drinking and laughter and banter and cheer.
But it's not quite where the story ends
What I found here, are lifelong friends.

And I know that nothing stays the same
Because life is an ever changing game,
There'll be new jobs, new homes and moving abroad,
Weddings and babies and new folk on board,
But right here, right now, I don't feel alone
Because when I walk in this pub I feel like I'm home.
It's the *heart* of Katie that pulls me back,
The wisdom, the wine, the jokes and the crack.
So thanks for befriending this silly old bird,
Even when I get all pissed and absurd
And in the future, I'd like you to be,
Still here in my life, not a memory.

Happy Birthday Sally & Simon

There are fifty ways to wish you happy birthday
Fifty wiles to commemorate the miles
And fifty styles to celebrate the smiles
And of course, fifty puns about reaching your half tonnes
But when I sat down to write, those thoughts took flight
And it didn't seem quite right
To trivialise tonight
So I won't make jokes about how Sally can't wait
To get Simon home on a Saturday night
Or about how we've sat up late
And watched them drink their body weights
Because, behind the jokes and the cheer
And the laughter and beer
Something quite wonderful starts to appear
It's absolutely crystal clear
That you hold each other very dear
They say good things come to those who wait
 And you've both been blessed by the hand of fate
And all the better for coming late
Because you recognised your soul mate
And it's obvious that you're on the right path
You only have to hear Sally's laugh
What a wonderful way to be
It's truly beautiful to see
The look of pride in Simon's eyes
When he looks at you Sally, there's no disguise
I know it hasn't always been this way
I know there have been dark days
Highs and lows and some life-blows
But your lives are now on a different track
You're going forward, not looking back
We can see your relationship is all about growth
And inner peace and love for you both

So Sally and Simon
Have a wonderful day
I'm sure you'll be laughing 'til you're old and grey
The next 50 years will be child's play
Live the life you want, do it your way
I know you will, anyway
Make fifty nifty, risky, and frisky
With love to you both
Happy birthday!

First World Thoughts When Stuck In Traffic 🚗 🚗 🚗 🚗 🚗

Should I shave off *all* my pubes, or leave a landing strip?
Does it matter anyway? Everyone's abandoned ship.
Will I have sex again or will my pussy just grow over?
Single and fifty, it's a genuine fear of growing older.

Is it too 80s to wear blue eyeliner?
Who will be the Glastonbury headliner?
I'll never get tickets, I'm in the office in those precious
minutes.
I could ask my assistant to attempt,
It couldn't possibly increase the contempt
In which she holds me.

Do I cook from scratch tonight or grab a Chinese or Indian?
Not literally,
I'm pretty sure grabbing ethnic people is politically incorrect.
Hey! Why didn't I get a cloverleaf on top of my latte?
The woman in front, *she* got a cloverleaf on top of her latte.
No, it's a maple leaf, sorry.
Ooh, do you know what I haven't had for ages?
Calamari.

That guy in the next lane is cute,
Oh, he's put down his window.
Unfortunately, it goes unheard,
There's so much traffic, I'm slightly deaf.
Should I smile and nod?
I cannot hear a bloody word.

Is he coming on to me, or being incredibly friendly?
He's *very* good looking, I have to say.

Oh, shit. Just realised. He's gay.
I thought it was too good to be *actually* true.
What is *actual* truth, anyway?
I *actually* don't know.

Who's that? Oh, a text from the ex.
Should I answer or make him wait?
I don't want to look too desperate.
We've been getting on with separate lives.
It's difficult with an ex.
Should I ask him round for sex?

This traffic! Should I merge left or right
Or stick it out in the middle lane?
It's like voting, left or right or straight down the middle.
Where is the middle, anyway?
Is speaking out on war and corruption cool or uncool?
Does *anyone* care anymore? Not politicians, it seems.
Yes! The glove box. A packet of custard creams.

I must remember to put out the bins,
Should I recycle or just chuck it all in?
Will my milk cartons change the environment?
Oh, shut up radio.
How about a bit of enlightenment?
Radio 4? No, fucking boring.
Ooh, what do we have on this station?
"David Bowie" (said in his voice).
Turn this shit up!
I love you David. Why did you die?

That guy! He's still looking. That must be his boyfriend.
Shit, just realised, the belt from my coat is hanging from the
door.
(Retrieve belt. Wave. Mouth, *"Thank you"*.)
Should I do something about the extinction of animals?

But how can I affect the plains of Africa?
I can't even afford Lanzarote.

Oh, look, the men are coming out the Mosque.
I like those white suits. Not sure about the trainers.
Which side of the holy war would I sit? I'm not even religious.
I'm pretty sure God dislikes me.
That's the last custard cream.
I might as well stop at McDonald's,
The diet's ruined anyway.

Where is my place in the universe?
Why am I here?
What happens when we die?
Oh, the traffic is moving,
Yes, free road, it's definitely improving.
It's taken twenty minutes to get out.
What the fuck have I been thinking about?

Morning on the Train

There's always a silver...
Lining my pockets with...
Money makes the world go...
Round and round, round and round
I never can finish the...
Line up! Line up!
Monday morning on the train,
I wonder when I'll go insane.
I'd meet you in the bluebell wood,
If I could.
If I could.

ROSE

A rose is a fragile thing,

Deadly yet delicate.

Step on it and it will die beneath your shoe,

Ignore it and it will parch to death,

Tear its petals, it will quiver, naked,

Just to pierce your heart with thorns

As you walk away.

The First Word

When there was nothing, nothing and nowhere,
just emptiness, unlit to earthly eyes,
no moon dictated to the oceans fair
or wingèd creatures crawled across the skies,
no leggèd beings swam along the earth,
or finnèd species walked the deep sea floor.
Reality trembled, waiting to give birth,
behind the universal door.
All was waiting for the spoken word,
to fragment into consciousness divine,
and, BANG! The word was spoken and we heard.
Gutted was the emptiness divine.
    The first word ever spoken took a knife
    and splintered us in sacred shards of life.

The Unicorn

Write what you know
Said a year 6 teacher
Don't make a feature
Of a mythical creature
Because you've never seen
A unicorn

You have twelve years
From the day you were born
Write about *that*
When you went to the sea
What you watch on TV
Write what you *see*

Not vampire bats
Or carnivorous rats
Madagascar cats
And circus acrobats
It's a little egocentric
And somewhat inauthentic

You don't live in a gypsy waggon
Drink mead from a silver flagon
And I know you didn't kill a dragon
Write what you see

That's the key,
If you want to be a writer

Behind him, on the wall
In a three dimensional sprawl
Is the world of my mind.
Jungles and oceans
And clothes with gold tassels
Flying carpets land
On fairytale castles
And through it all
With its great gilded horn
strides a mighty silver unicorn

So I turn the page upon my knee
And write what I can see

Dead Cold
############

I'm sat in a station waiting room,
I'm counting the seconds, my dear,
I'm hungry and thirsty and cold as the tomb,
Too numb to shed a tear.

Anonymous train, please come for me,
Slide open your carriage door,
Convey me to the tragedy
Fate always had in store.

I'm now in the grimy, growling train,
Each second you are dearer,
The rains are my teardrops converged on the pane,
Each second brings you nearer.

Soon, I will hold you close, my dear,
And kiss your face and your cold, closed eyes,
I'll climb on the slab and hold you,
As I did before you died.

Why?

Why are we not guardians
Of every living thing,
Animals and creatures
Of sea and land and wing?

We eat them, beat them,
Carve them and starve them,
Keep them in cages
And parade them on stages.

We clone them; disown them
Rein them and chain them
Hunt them with guns,
Just to have fun.

We trap them, we scrap them,
Experiment to their detriment,
Bash them with clubs
And orphan their cubs.

For pity's sake, I do deplore,
Let's not do this anymore.

Slip Inside Me

Don't bore me
Explore me
Inside me, there's a candy store
And in my bottom drawer
There's so much more, much more

Don't paw me
Adore me
Within me, lies a huge bookstore
And should knowledge become a chore
The librarian is a whore

Don't score me
Look for me
In the body writhing on the floor
If you look into my core
You'll find warrior, friend and mentor

Don't ignore me
Implore me
To open up my arcane door
And spew my secrets on the floor
Where you could sit for evermore

Come in through the front door
Or slip in through the back
There's more to me than skin and bone
There's more to me, much more to me
Slip inside and see

Life Imitates Art

I'm a thinker in an unmade bed,
Staring up to a starry night,
I block visions of a flaming June
As I wait for the painter of light.

And yet, the memories persist,
I feel all the love and pain.
I picture you buying me sunflowers
In a Paris street in the rain

Or handing me pearl earrings
By the water lily pond,
A faint impression of sunrise
On the landscape with snow beyond.

Now, I cannot tell if you are smiling
For all is a lavender mist,
The warmth has left our embrace
And the world is as cold as your kiss.

I reach for you but my arms feel broken
Was it all a dream?
In silence, we eat our last supper,
Inside, I can hear myself scream.

Elliott ♥♥♥

We run inside to miss the rain
Chloe's on the bar again
The year moved on, it's different weather
Since you left the pub forever
Halloween and bonfire night
Tuesday quiz and open mic
Laughter on the smoking deck
Coats on now and scarves round necks
No flowers on the fireplace
No pictures left to show your face
And while we rarely mention you
In silences you take your cue
To move back to your place and find
Your seat with those you left behind
You listen to our idle natter
Opinions on things that matter
And things that matter not a bit
Drinks in hands and cigarettes lit
You're still a part of all of it
And though it seems like we moved on
We don't forget that someone's gone
And when we least expect the pain
It pours on us like Autumn rain

23828651R00066

Printed in Great Britain
by Amazon